GETTING OUT OF THE BOAT
BREAKING FREE FROM DOUBT AND WALKING BY FAITH INTO YOUR DESTINY

VERA MUNFUS

Getting Out of the Boat: Breaking Free from Doubt and Walking by Faith into Your Destiny

Copyright © 2025 Vera Munfus

All rights reserved. No part of this book may be reproduced, stored, or transmitted by any means- whether auditory, graphic, mechanical, or electronic without the publisher's and author's written permission, except in the case of brief excerpts used in critical articles and reviews. The unauthorized reproduction of any part of this work is illegal and punishable by law.

Unless otherwise notated, scripture quotations are taken from the Holy Bible, New Living Translation, copyright ©1996, 2004, 2015 by Tyndale House Foundation. Used by permission of Tyndale House Publishers, Carol Stream, Illinois 60188. All rights reserved. Printed and bound in the United States of America

Book Creation and Design
Brand It Beautifully™
www.branditbeautifully.com

ISBN for Paperback version: ISBN: 979-8-218-70017-1

Printed in the United States of America

DEDICATION

*To every soul who's ever felt the fear of stepping out—
may you find the courage to trust God anyway.
This is for the water-walkers.*

TABLE OF CONTENTS

Introduction	vii
AN AMAZING OUT-OF-BODY EXPERIENCE Vera Munfus	1
PURPOSE GETS YOU OUT OF THE BOAT Barbara Council	13
I'M STILL HERE Bernadette Flakes	21
GOD'S GOT THIS Brenda Simpson	25
WHEN GOD'S PLANS ARE DIFFERENT FROM YOURS Bridget Wells	35
JOURNEY TO FREEDOM Carolyn R. Inman	45
MOVE FROM FAITH TO FAITH Debra Cofer	53
WORKING OUT MY PURPOSE Glenda D. Richardson	63
HE WILL NEVER LEAVE YOU Linda Denmark-Austin	73
ANCHOR OF FAITH Ollie L. Lofton	81
YOU MUST GET OUT OF THE BOAT Dr. Sharon E. Harris	91

INTRODUCTION

There comes a moment in every believer's life when the boat no longer feels like home. It's familiar, yes—but it's also confining. Deep down, you know you were made for more. You hear the whisper of God calling you out onto the waters, inviting you into something greater than comfort, something deeper than safety: a life fully surrendered in faith. That's what this book is about.

Getting Out of the Boat is not just a title—it's a personal challenge. It's a call to move from fear to faith, from stagnation to purpose, from questioning to obedience. Inspired by the story of Peter walking on water, this book captures the essence of what it means to trust God beyond logic, beyond limitations, and beyond what feels "safe."

Inside these pages, you'll find stories from real people who took bold steps of faith in their own lives. Some were terrified. Some doubted. All were transformed. These

INTRODUCTION

testimonies aren't perfect, polished success stories—they are raw, honest, and deeply human accounts of what happens when ordinary people dare to believe in an extraordinary God.

You'll meet people who:

- Said yes to God when it didn't make sense
- Let go of comfort to walk in calling
- Faced fear, failure, and uncertainty—but kept moving
- Discovered that Jesus never leaves you on the water alone

Whether you're standing at the edge of your next decision or struggling to hear God in the storm, this book is for you.

Let it be your permission to let go of the boat.

Let it be your encouragement to take the first step.

Let it be your reminder that faith isn't about perfection—it's about movement.

You won't have all the answers. But you do have Jesus.

And that's more than enough.

So take a deep breath.

This is your moment.

Let's get out of the boat.

AN AMAZING OUT-OF-BODY EXPERIENCE
VERA MUNFUS

Have you ever wondered what God's plans and purpose are for you in death? I've read in scripture that it is appointed to man once to die and then the judgement. So, we know that to leave this earth, we will have to die. I had no preconceived notions about how I would leave this earth. What was evident, as a believer, was one, I would die and live to talk about it. Or two, I would die a regular death and be translated into heaven. One could never prepare for any of these occurrences. So let me tell my story.

My story began during a business trip to Orlando, Florida. I woke up that morning with abdominal pain. I knew I was not going to be able to attend this meeting. I took the next flight back to Houston, making an appointment with my doctor. She gave me the diagnosis that I had large gallstones in my gallbladder that could not be removed through laser surgery. This would require the removal of the entire gallbladder. After discussing the procedure with the doctor, talking to friends that had their gallbladder removed, I was somewhat comforted knowing that it was not something too major. After going into much prayer, I was comforted in knowing that God had a plan for me, even though I did not yet know what it was.

Well, the surgery was a success, or so I thought. After a couple of days, I was preparing to be discharged. During those couple of days, what I didn't know was that I was hemorrhaging every time I went to the restroom. Which meant I was losing blood each time I used the restroom. Nevertheless, the doctor proceeded with preparing my discharge papers. One of the ministers from my church came out to visit and pray with me that evening before I was going to be released a few hours later. During his prayer, I had a witness by the Holy Spirit to stay another night. This was also followed by an uncomfortable feeling in my stomach. So, I asked my doctor if I could stay another day. I knew this was the Holy Spirit because I had placed the entire procedure in God's hands. My trust was in His guidance and protection. He would lead and guide me. Every step required was in God's hand. My dependence was not in the wisdom of doctors, but my trust was in the power of the word of God, my healer. **Psalms 12:2 says Heaven and earth will pass away, but my words will never pass away.** So, they allowed me to stay another day. Look at God! When the nurse came in, I mentioned to her what was happening in the restroom, and she seemed alarmed. She told me if that happened again to make sure I called the nursing station and ask for her. Well, it happened again a few hours later, around 1:00am in the morning. As I entered the restroom and sat down, I felt a heavy flow of liquid flowing from my body. Suddenly, I felt very weak, losing consciousness. I tried to grab the call button as I was falling. My head hit the floor very hard. I noticed that I didn't really feel any pain from the fall. In a split second, my body began to rise upward toward the ceiling. Things happened too fast for me to process what was going on. As I was moving upward, I noticed a body lying on the floor. To my surprise, I realized the body on the floor was mine. Normally, I am a person who expresses my thoughts, ideas, and opinions out loud. However, I could not speak with my mouth, my spirit was clearly talking. I even acknowledged that the body I was looking at was mine. Oh, my goodness! I realized what was happening to me. I DIED! At that point, everything I ever read in the bible made sense. The scriptures flooded my spirit, seemingly filling the atmosphere. I understood that God's word had the power to reproduce in my life what doctors could not because they were not present. All I could hear was scriptures I had either read or meditated on that were coming up in my spirit. **Psalms 118:17 "I will live and not die and declare the works of the Lord" (Psalms 91:11) "For He will command his angels concerning you to guard you in all your ways."** I clearly heard the Lord speaking to my spirit clearer than if He was talking to me face to face. It seemed like the more I heard the word, the closer I moved back to coming into my body. I knew I was not ready to go home to be with the Lord. Ironically, I also didn't believe that it was God's will for me to return home just yet either. When I came back into my body, I heard the nurse come on the intercom asking if I needed help. Because there was no response from me, I could hear her say, "Oh my God, she's in trouble."

They rushed to my room and into the restroom. They picked me up off the floor. They started inserting tubes down my throat and nose, IVs in my arms, and giving me several pints of blood transfusions. Tubes were everywhere. I was in a lot of pain. But the word of the Lord kept coming. I heard the Lord say, **"I will uphold you with my right hand."** Immediately, I felt someone holding my hand. Thinking that the nurse was holding my hand, I struggled to look down to confirm. But there was no one holding my hand.

It's recorded in scripture that His word will not return void. The scripture also states that He sent His word, and it healed. So, the word has so much power, yet we don't exercise our right to use its power. The word releases health and life when you believe and speak it. We're living in a time where the enemy, our adversary, is using all platforms to control our minds (what we think), our will (what we will do or not do), our emotions (how we feel), our imagination (what we can dream or envision), and our intellect (what we can create, design, or build). This is the boat we may be living in that has become our comfort zone. Our belief system has been shaped by our traditional upbringing, life experiences, credible authority we trust, and educational training over the years. I must add social media platforms that tend to shape our thinking of what is real and what is not real. Nevertheless, these types of influences can cause us to develop a comfort zone that we are afraid to venture outside of. This opens the door for the fear of the unknown to set in, limiting our potential to glorify God, grow in our faith, and fulfill our purpose. As a result, we risk dying prematurely—spiritually, emotionally, or even physically —before our time. We have been given authority in the earth realm, and it's ours to use.

As I laid there in the bed with both of my arms and hands stretched out, I could feel markings resembling crosses being carved in both of my hands. I could only imagine the sufferings Christ suffered for me. Let me paint a picture of what I was dealing with in that hospital room. I had tubes down my esophagus and nose. Therefore, I could not talk or even move. It hurt so badly to swallow. So, I dreaded each moment I had to swallow. There were IVs running in both of my arms and one in my hand. I was in excruciating pain. Even in all this aftermath, I still pondered on the purpose and how this would glorify my heavenly Father. Through it all, I was prepared to endure what was ahead of me. What happened that caused me to go into hemorrhaging was the question I wanted answered. What I later discovered was during the initial surgery, a piece of my lung had been accidentally clipped —and it was not revealed.

They transported me to the ICU unit to be scheduled for surgery the following morning. Surgery was to repair the damage that was done to the portion of my lungs, which caused me to hemorrhage. Hopefully, this would stop the bleeding.

How many times have you found yourself at a crossroads questioning God for the purpose of this trial or test? One thing I was sure of was that I trusted my heavenly Father to bring me through.

All that night, I endured the discomfort of not being able to talk or barely swallow. The only thing that brought consolation was knowing I could meditate on the scriptures—and I did so with deep confidence and assurance that the Father was hearing me. The Spirit of the Lord brought to my remembrance the following scriptures: *"I will not die but live and will proclaim what the Lord has done."* (**Rom. 14:8 NIV**); *"But I was young and now I am old, yet I have never seen the righteous forsaken, or their children begging bread"* (**Psalms 37:25 NIV**). And because I was also thinking about my husband and children and what they were going through, thinking that they were going to lose their mother and his wife: *"No one will be able to stand against you all the days of your life. As I was with Moses, so I will be with you; I will never leave you nor forsake you." (Joshua 1:5 NIV)*

As I meditated on these scriptures, I could hear a loud cry coming from an adjacent hospital room. It was a man crying for help. He cried all night long. No one came to check on him. Feeling very heartbroken for him, and the incompetency of the staff to care for him, I meditated on the scripture that says, *"For he will command his angels*

AN AMAZING OUT-OF-BODY EXPERIENCE

concerning you to guard you in all your ways." (**Psalms 91:11 NIV**).

Early that morning around 3:00am or 4:00am, a nurse attendant came in to run another IV with medication to prep me for the surgery. I wondered why I was getting new medicine at this time without a doctor coming in to see me and discussing the reason for the change in medication. For some reason, this nurse attendant had the most difficult time inserting the needle into my veins to run the IV. I knew I had small veins, but this was ridiculous. The pain was unbearable at times; but my trust was still in the Lord. His frustration was evident as he left the room. He only returned momentarily to retrieve my chart. What was not apparent to me was my mother, Jessie Brown, who lives in Orlando, FL, made a phone call to the hospital at that exact time. She asked to be transferred to the Nursing Station across from my room. She spoke to the head nurse attendant, explaining to her who she was, who she was calling for, and what her qualifications were in the medical field. She asked her to get my chart and read it to her. She stated that she understood medical terms and what she didn't understand, she had access to accurate interpretation by skilled doctors. What they didn't know was my mother had worked in the hospital for 40 years around some of the best doctors in the United States. When she read my chart to her, she questioned the medication that was about to be administered through the IV. She explained to the nurse attendant the harm that prescribed medication would do to me. My mother told her that was the wrong medication to give a patient with my diagnoses. She demanded the name and phone number of the doctor on call, who was asleep at home. All of this was transpiring without my knowledge. Around 5:00am the doctor comes into my room and says, "You have an extraordinary mother!" He shared the story with me about how my mother called him at 4:00am in the morning. He stated how she insisted he return to the hospital because I was about to be given the wrong medication. She wanted to know who prescribed it and the purpose for running the IV. He was so intrigued by her knowledge and understanding of medical terminology. My mother was that angel that God commanded to take charge over me to keep me from falling. I'm grateful that I had a mother who was praying for me; who was not afraid to get out of the boat and challenge the system. In fact, she rocked the boat that morning.

This experience changed my life forever. Simply put, walking by faith in the word of God—and not by sight—is the authority we've been given to live by. Trust the God of your salvation, who has given you everything that pertains to life. He's made you righteous through the blood of Jesus. He's given you the measure of faith to use to make a spiritual transfer from heaven to your situation. He has not given you a spirit of fear, but love, power, and a sound mind. So, you *can* do all things through Christ, who gives you the strength to do it. You have been graced in this hour and given truth to make the right decision.

Peter was doing fine until he took his eyes off Jesus and began looking at the waves and turning his attention to how hard the wind was blowing. It was only then that he began to sink. There's power in the word of God. Let that be your meditation so that when you're facing big waves and hard winds, you can confidently speak the word of God—the very word that will get you out of the boat!

MEET THE AUTHOR | VERA MUNFUS

Vera Munfus is a retired educator. One of her passions is serving others in the Kingdom of God. She has been active in her community, participating in Habitat for Humanity programs where she helped to build homes for less fortunate others.

Mrs. Munfus was formally educated at the University of Central Florida in Orlando, Florida and the University of St. Thomas in Houston, Texas. She has 30 years' experience in education from grade school to college and a myriad of awards and accomplishments in that field. She has served as a public-school teacher, Librarian, GT coordinator, test coordinator and teacher specialist. She possesses a B.A. Degree in Business Education, certifications in Elementary Education, and English as a Second Language.

Mrs. Munfus is also a graduate of the Light Christian Institute of Ministry, Ministers Development Institute,

Graduate Advance Studies Program, and Leadership Academy. She taught Light Bible Institute courses and Graduate Advance Studies Program courses for 10 years at the New Light Christian Center Church. She was ordained as a Pastor by Bishop I.V. Hilliard at New Light Christian Center. Mrs. Munfus taught Marriage and Orientation/Membership Classes there for six years. She served faithfully 26 years in ministry at New Light Christian Center.

Mrs. Munfus enrolled and graduated from The School of Deliverance Ministry under the founder, Hazel Hughes. She joined the Hazel Hughes School of Deliverance Ministry as an instructor, receiving her Minister's Ordination License in 2005. She taught courses at Hazel Hughes School of Deliverance Ministry at the University of Houston for four years, seeing many receive their minister's certification.

Mrs. Munfus joined Fresh Impact Church in 2015 in the beginning stages of its foundation before its launching. She was ordained as a Prophetess in 2023. She actively serves on the pastoral team, prayer partners team, and leads the Intercessory Team Ministry. She is Dream Team Captain over Next Steps.

Although Mrs. Munfus husband, Timothy Sr. of 39 years passed in 2021. They're the proud parents of four amazing children, Timothy Jr., DeMarcus, Ashley, and Briana. She also has one daughter-in-law, Claressa, and one beautiful granddaughter, Aubrey at the time of this writing.

Mrs. Munfus enjoys fulfilling her purpose in life through ministry and education, spending time with her family and helping others to achieve their highest potential. She gets much pleasure in developing others spiritually, educationally, mentally and emotionally.

PURPOSE GETS YOU OUT OF THE BOAT
BARBARA COUNCIL

On my birthday, March 16, 2000, my good friend, my play cousin-in-law, gave me a prayer journal. The inscription said, "Barbara, may your blessings be abundant now and always. Love, Rena." Rena has been a great prayer warrior in my life and family. The title of the prayer journal was *The Power Of A Praying Woman* and includes reflections throughout from Stormie Omartian. I waited over a year to write in my journal and made my first entry on March 30, 2001. The first thing I wrote in this journal was a list of people, places, and things to pray over. Stormie stated, *"There is something powerful about writing our prayers and concerns. It forces us to think clearly about what the deepest desires of our heart really are. It's a way of communicating with God."* So when we write our prayers out, we can thank God afterward on how He answers them. I wrote the following prayer requests: *God, strengthen my faith and help me achieve a closer prayer life with You.* Also, I included prayers over my marriage, children, parents, siblings, relatives, friends, co-workers, schools, and the nation. Everything I listed, I followed with *"help me achieve a closer prayer life with You."* Everything I listed and asked for, God answered. The following are testaments to how things began shifting once I started writing in my prayer journal.

God tested my faith on April 3, 2001. During a time when my marriage was strained, my husband asked me to go on a lunch date, but I couldn't go because of a mandatory meeting at work. I should have thanked him for asking, but I didn't. I always seem to think of the right thing to say after the moment has passed.

To reaffirm my faith in God, I was invited to a women's conference by a co-worker on Saturday, May 5, 2001—my second oldest child's birthday. So many of the things I had been struggling with were addressed during that conference: marriage (and the possibility of divorce), my relationship with my kids, spending quality time in God's presence, and the everyday struggles of life.

Later that day, I surprised my daughter with a birthday cake after she won her basketball game. She turned 18 years old. The cake had two pictures of her—one as an infant, and one as a young teenager. Galatians 6:9–10.

On May 6, 2001, I received a love letter from my husband. At the time, I had been struggling to keep up with my Experiencing God class, especially with reading my lessons, because of my heavy workload.

Then on May 9, 2001, I had a "powwow" with my 18-year-old daughter and 13-year-old son about household chores. I told them how they didn't seem to appreciate their blessings. That same day, I also had a conference call with my manager because I had refused to drive through a storm late at night to see a hospice patient. Thankfully, it went better than expected—a true testimony of God's grace.

On May 16, 2001, I expressed to God that I was starting to feel better about my marriage and that I knew our kids needed great role models. I spent time reminiscing, flipping through a photo album filled with memories from my wedding, our children, family, and friends.

I wrote to God, *"I know I need to pray more and ask for Your understanding about what's going on with me and in my life."* I held onto *Isaiah 1:19*: *"If you are willing and obedient, you will eat the good things of the land."*

Back in 1978, I stepped out in faith and left my comfort zone. I left behind my immediate family, relatives, and friends to move to Dallas, Texas, with my boyfriend of two years. God blessed me with a beautiful marriage in 1980 after dating him for five years—we had met when I was just 16 years old.

I earned my nursing degree, had three beautiful children, and later, six wonderful grandchildren. I built a fulfilling, though sometimes challenging, career and enjoyed a strong family life—until July 1, 2014.

That's when God tested my faith again with the passing of my husband due to Stage 4 pancreatic cancer. We started attending church as a family. All three of my children got baptized together when they were younger. After my husband was diagnosed with cancer, he got baptized again, and his desire to live became stronger. He lived 22 months after his diagnosis, which was unusual for the type of cancer he had. I thanked God for allowing my husband to be with us that long, but it didn't make us any more prepared for his death.

After the passing of my husband, I fell into a deep depression. I had a complete meltdown at the airport while traveling back to Florida to visit my family, in-laws, friends, and other close relatives. I was overwhelmed with grief and even thought about ending my life—I wondered how I would do it.

But through it all, my church family, God, and the counselors from the hospice team helped me renew my faith. I realized I couldn't leave my kids, grandkids, relatives, and friends behind. My husband would want me to carry on—and to continue living out his legacy.

So, in November 2023, I had stepped out in faith once again. The very husband who took me from Orlando in life, brought me back to Orlando through his passing—so I could care for my elderly mother.

The pain of losing him became my purpose. To carry out the plan and purpose God had for me, I had to get out of the boat.

PURPOSE GETS YOU OUT OF THE BOAT

Most times, in pain, God is preparing us to be a blessing to someone else. Because of this, you must surround yourself with people who will support your gifts. And on top of that, release the people who speak to you from their limitations because they keep you bound because they are. For example, if you receive a diagnosis of Diabetes, you want people around you that will say, *"God is going to heal you,"* and not the ones who will say, *"Girl, you better take your meds."* Examine the people who are in your space and be determined to live your best life and show up as your best self.

Your purpose is often birthed from your pain. What purpose is your pain birthing in you? I challenge you to get out of the boat and step into your purpose.

MEET THE AUTHOR | BARBARA COUNCIL

Born in Orlando, Florida, Barbara Council has proudly called Texas home for over four decades. After marrying her high school sweetheart, she poured her heart into raising their three children—while simultaneously building a career rooted in compassion, purpose, and service to others.

A proud graduate of Texas Woman's University with a Bachelor's degree in Nursing, Barbara has spent her professional life making a meaningful difference in the lives of those she cares for. Guided by a deep Christian faith, she has faithfully served on the Stewardess Board at Christian Chapel Temple of Faith for more than 20 years.

Barbara's commitment to community shines through her involvement with a number of civic and faith-based organizations, including the Orlando Voters League, Voices For Our Fathers Legacy Foundation, and Texas Faith Community Nursing.

When she's not serving others, Barbara treasures time with her wonderful family—cheering on her three children and seven grandchildren at their games, performances, and life's big moments. In 2024, Barbara joined Lift Orlando as one of the inaugural Senior Ambassadors, a select group of four entrusted with launching a pilot program aimed at supporting young readers experiencing difficulties.

I'M STILL HERE
BERNADETTE FLAKES

Bernadette is my given name, but family and friends call me Bernie. I grew up in the city of Brotherly Love—Philadelphia, PA. I have had several challenges with getting out of the boat. I pray that what I'm about to share will offer hope and courage to any woman who may be facing—or has faced—similar situations to mine.

I have a chronic disease called Sickle Cell Anemia, which is a disease of the blood that causes tremendous pain throughout the body and most of the time requires blood transfusions and doses of opioids. It is an inherited disease and cannot be caught or transmitted. Living in a cold climate led to many painful episodes of "crisis" and hospitalization. A crisis happens when a person with Sickle Cell gets too cold, gets overly stressed, or doesn't drink enough water during the day to prevent blood cells from clotting. My doctor advised me that as I got older, my episodes would increase. Therefore, he suggested I move to a warmer climate, like Florida.

So, with his suggestion, I moved. That was my first challenge of getting out of the boat—being brave enough to take my doctor's advice and move to a warmer climate where I knew no one. I built up my courage and moved to Florida, with my sister coming with me for support and encouragement. I was blessed to get a job working with the airlines, hiding my illness from and experiencing fewer episodes with my health.

My second challenge of getting out of the boat was leaving the man I married after moving to Florida. After enduring 10 years of affairs, sexually transmitted diseases, and verbal abuse, I finally made the decision to leave him.Upon deciding to leave, and building up the courage, I made the move. While packing my things to leave, he came home and told me I wasn't leaving nor divorcing him. He put a gun to my head and threatened to shoot me and himself. At that moment, I said a prayer and told him if he was going to shoot me, then there was nothing I could do, so do it. I pleaded the Blood of Jesus! He dropped the gun and told me to leave. I left and filed for divorce and with God's grace; I survived. He stalked me for about a year until I moved to another part of Florida.

My third challenge of getting out of the boat was battling a severe crisis while slipping in and out of consciousness and maintaining my willpower to continue living. I was in the boat of death dealing with a Sickle Cell crisis, double pneumonia, and a ruptured gallbladder. The doctor told my family that it was touch and go and that I had to have the willpower to fight if I wanted to live. Going in and out of consciousness and hearing bits and pieces of conversations with doctors coming in and out of my room with their diagnosis and doubts about me surviving, I decided I wanted to live and not die. I remember lying in my hospital bed and asking God to give me the willpower to want to live. By God's grace and mercy, with my mind set on living, God brought me through.

And by His grace...I'm still here!

My favorite Bible verse, Proverbs 3:5-6 says, "***Trust in the Lord with all thy heart and lean not unto thy own understanding. In all thy ways acknowledge Him and He will direct thy path.***" When you are struggling to find the will to survive, I encourage you to remember that scripture and repeat my favorite affirmation: ***I am blessed and highly favored of the Lord.*** With God's help, you *can* get out of whatever boat you find yourself in—and you must because you belong here!

MEET THE AUTHOR | BERNADETTE "BERNIE" FLAKES

Bernadette "Bernie" Flakes was born and raised in Philadelphia, Pennsylvania, and later moved to Orlando, Florida, for health reasons. A divorcee and proud mother of one son, Bernie has been an entrepreneur with Mary Kay Cosmetics for over 20 years. Deeply committed to community service, she is passionate about helping others and making a lasting impact.

She is a member of Gamma Delta Sorority of Eatonville, Florida, and serves as Vice President of the Board of Directors at Oak Shadows Condominiums. Bernie was also instrumental in forming the nonprofit organization Sickle Cell Conquerors of Central Florida, created to support individuals living with sickle cell disease and to educate communities about the condition.

Bernie is honored to be part of this incredible women's ministry, continuing her lifelong mission of service, empowerment, and faith.

GOD'S GOT THIS
BRENDA SIMPSON

> *Blessed is the man who walks not in the counsel of the ungodly, nor stands in the path of sinners, sits in the seat of the scornful; But his delight is in the law of the Lord, and in his law, he meditates day and night. He shall be like a tree planted by the rivers of water. That brings forth its fruit in its season, whose leaf also shall not wither and whatever he does shall prosper.*
>
> — PSALM 1:1-3

God made everybody different. My struggles haven't been hard—just a bit challenging. The next couple of statements are bringing me to tears, because I need for you to know something about *me*, Brenda Simpson. I went to the doctor to get tested, and they had a name for my challenge—dyslexia. It turns out dyslexia is linked to certain genes that affect how the brain processes reading and language.

I interact with people daily, but I am different from other people. I have dyslexia. Now that I have said it, I hope you don't have a different opinion of me. If so, I pray you're able to move past it. Despite my differences, I met a wonderful man who married me and accepted me as I am. My husband told me that his grandfather was just like me—and it was okay. When you are in love, it is a blessing from God.

My husband, Roy, has reminded me many times how intelligent I am. His motivation has inspired me in many ways, especially in running my business call *Daycare Plus*. I ran Daycare Plus for many years. One year, I opened and ran a daycare for Forest Hill Community Bible Church. After that, I went back home and continued to run my own business. I attended Tarrant County College and Weatherford College, to maintain my day care licenses and to take classes for my business. One thing I know is—as long as we live in the world, we are going to have problems that come against us, but God's word instructs us and shows us the ways to face these problems and guide us through them. And this is what he has done for me over and over in my life. Even with dyslexia, I was able to have my own business and work for myself.

Roy and I have two wonderful daughters. Tina Simpson, my first daughter, and I were in an abusive marriage. I cried out to the Lord to help me and one day Tina, a baby at the time, said to me, "Mommy, don't cry. I love you."

This inspired me to ask the Lord to get me out of this boat of abuse. God used Tina to save my life.

Andrea Tubbs, my youngest daughter, keeps me on my toes. Andrea helped keep me grounded like the "prodigal child" (Luke15:11-32). Andrea is the mother of three of my grandchildren and Jared Tubbs, my son-in-law, gave me two more. I am so grateful for them all.

When the pandemic came, I was just getting over the loss of my son-in-law, Jared Tubbs. God took him home to be with Him at an early age. The pandemic took us in a different direction and we had to get together as a family to figure out this new way of life. How to keep safe, how to not destroy each other, and how to be in a house together 24 hours a day. Andrea and the family produced good ideas for the family—Bible time, games, all kinds of card games, dominos, puzzles, food recipes, watching movies, reading books, and more.

One day, I got a call from Debra Cofer, my cousin from Orlando, FL, to be on a prayer line on Sunday. She said the Lord led her to start it. I was happy to be a support, so I joined. Normally, I'm not doing anything on Sunday at the time the prayer call starts, so around 5 o'clock I was available.

I have enjoyed the prayer line every Sunday since. We pray together, cry together, and encourage each other. I have had years of challenges. I am looking forward to all the new challenges. What follows is how one of my challenges tried to keep me in the boat.

Worrying about things out of my control, I called Deb, and I told her I could not go to the ladies prayer retreat. I had paid for the prayer retreat and the Williams Family Reunion, which was scheduled for the same weekend.

Deb replied, "Stop, just stop. God's got this." When you have doubts about things, that is when you know you need to pray and listen to God, because he already knows.

We prayed about the retreat—that maybe the dates would change, and God blessed us. The dates for the retreat and reunion changed. Look at God! I was meant to be at that retreat! My husband, Roy, drove me to Orlando, FL for the first retreat and I was able to meet the ladies I had been praying with on the phone and put faces with names and voices.

One of the first things I did was see Carolyn Inman and give her a big hug. She is one of the ladies I invited on the prayer line, my friend, for over 50 years. I would babysit her son, Calvin, when she lived in Sacramento, CA. Carolyn was an Air Force member, and I was an Air Force wife. I then made my way around, hugging the other sisters and putting faces with the names.

I really enjoyed that first evening of officially meeting one another. And you know what's funny? I found out I had been praying with my cousin Ollie this whole time and didn't even know it! While I was talking with one lady, Ollie looked around and said, "Is your mama called Mutt?"

I said, "Yes, I'm your cousin from Ocala." We had not seen each other since we were kids. I knew this was the work of God.

I can remember writing self-encouragement words and recognizing that my strength is holding on to God's promises; His goodness to me. That night we were giggling like little young ladies enjoying our time together, the food, the laughter, the joyful crying, and just being silly. Psalm 30:5 says, *"Weeping may endure for a night, but joy come in the morning."* Joy was in the air, and I could see God's hand in the middle of all I was doing. Carolyn and I made sure we involved ourselves with the other ladies as much as we could.

The next day, we all woke up early, excited to get together. We greeted each other, looking at the beautiful breakfast that was prepared. The joy, laughter, and warm greetings were such a blessing. The Holy Spirit was in the room.

As the music was played, Sister Pam told us the agenda for the day. Prophetess Vera taught a class called, *"If You Want to Walk on Water, You Got to Get Out of the Boat."* She shared Jesus told Peter to come to Him and Peter stepped out of the boat and walked on the water, but started to sink when he became afraid of the waves. I do this often—take my focus off God and find myself stuck in the boat or sinking.

It was during this presentation and activity that I truly saw myself. I recalled how people have always told me about my personality—how smart I am and how they like to be around me. I am a gift from God, spoken humbly, of course. But I didn't see it before. I wanted to walk boldly in my gifts from God, so I asked the Holy Spirit to guide me in all I do.

For helping step out of the boat of doubting the gift of God in me, I first would like to thank Roy Simpson for being a godly man who leads his family in continuing to praise the Lord.

Thank you, Debra, for calling me to join the prayer line and encouraging me to pray when it's my time. To Sister Vera—thank you for walking me out of the boat and always speaking encouragement into my life.

God, You made each of us different, and I thank You for that. You are the reason I live a blessed life. You are the reason I have wonderful daughters and why my grandchildren continue to thrive, even after the loss of their father.

God, I give You all the praise and all the glory. Sister Vera once told me I am wonderfully made by You, and no matter what I'm going through, You will bring me through it. I have learned from these experiences and I pray I can bless the people that You place in my path.

God, this has been an awesome experience. I'm so grateful to be able to write these words to bless other people. My goal is to be the person You have called me to be.

Even at my age, there's still so much to learn. But You have already taught me so much—how to be a wonderful wife, a devoted mother and grandmother, and a true friend.

I've had a wonderful life. I've lived in a different country, traveled across the United States, and formed meaningful bonds with people from all over. I've been blessed with a wonderful mother and father, and caring sisters and brothers.

Staying out of the boat—choosing faith over fear—is what we must continue to focus on. Let God's guidance lead you in all aspects of life: how to live, how to treat others, how to love, and how to forgive.

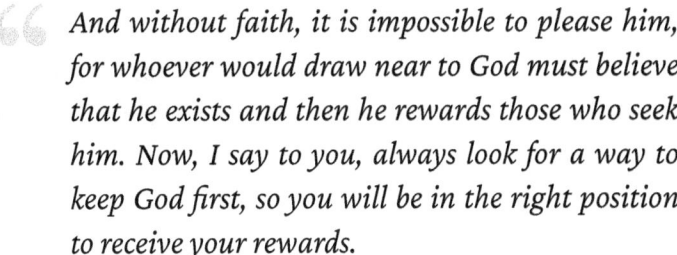

> *And without faith, it is impossible to please him, for whoever would draw near to God must believe that he exists and then he rewards those who seek him. Now, I say to you, always look for a way to keep God first, so you will be in the right position to receive your rewards.*
>
> — HEBREWS 11:6

MEET THE AUTHOR | BRENDA SIMPSON

Brenda Simpson is a devoted woman of faith who cherishes her family and the blessings in her life. She is married to her "Christmas man," Roy Simpson, and is the proud mother of two beautiful daughters, Tina Simpson and Andrea Tubbs. Brenda is also a loving grandmother to five wonderful grandchildren: Jamiah, Jaedon, twins Jeremiah and Janyiah, and the youngest, Sarai. Though her family has faced loss, including her beloved son-in-law, Jarrod Tubbs, who was called home at a young age, Brenda's faith and gratitude remain steadfast.

For over 30 years, Brenda owned and was the Director of her own daycare center, a passion inspired by her love for children. She also opened the daycare as a ministry through Forest Hill Community Bible Church in Fort Worth, Texas, where it served the community for over two decades. Alongside running her daycare, Brenda also worked as a caregiver and hairdresser for the children she cared for.

Outside of her professional accomplishments, Brenda has a deep love for real estate and enjoys a variety of hobbies, including bowling, puzzles, and spending time at the beach. She treasures moments with her family, entertaining friends, and cooking delicious meals. An avid traveler, Brenda has explored nearly all 50 states and dreams of visiting the remaining few. She also loves cruises and taking road trips with loved ones.

Brenda is a woman who radiates gratitude and joy, embracing life's blessings with an open heart. She gives thanks to the Lord for guiding her journey and enriching her life in countless ways.

WHEN GOD'S PLANS ARE DIFFERENT FROM YOURS
BRIDGET WELLS

I am one of six siblings, and our parents were migrant workers that lived eight months in the North and four months in the South. Each child traveled until they began high school. We were in slavery in the 70s and didn't even know it. We lived in a migrant camp in the North and my father was the foreman; he was the only one allowed to bring his children. We were the only children in the camp. My parents worked from sunup to sundown six days a week with no time off for doctors' visits or to run errands or do hardly anything other than work. My mother had a miscarriage in the field and her friend put the baby in her lunch bag and my mother kept working. We took turns staying home from school to keep our younger siblings while my parents worked because they had no babysitter.

My parents picked apples, cherries, and pears while living in the North. However, my father made a way to make money other than picking fruit for the white man. He saved the money from the pool hall that he created out of a barn that was beneath where we lived. He was smart and had great money sense; he knew how to talk to people, and they were easily to be befriended by him. In the South, we owned our own home; my parents would bring back the money they would make from the pool hall and enhance our way of living while we were in the South. My parents did not believe in banks, they kept most of their money under the mattress. Neither of my parents graduated from high school and in fact my mother had a 9th grade education, and my father had an even lesser education, but one could not tell in having a conversation with them. They instilled strong working habits within us, and we carried that with us to adulthood. My parents protected us as much as they could, and I thank them for the protection that they provided, but it was not enough. I was raped at a young age; I never discussed it with my parents. I got pregnant at 15 and my daughter got pregnant at 13. This is my story and how I got out of the boat.

Our family goal was to break the generational cycle of teenage pregnancy, and we have done it thus far. The last two generations, there were no teenage pregnancies. Another one of our family goals was college. I was the first in my family to graduate from college and there have been many more after me. It was not easy getting out of the boat. I was afraid to show my true self because life's circumstances impacted me a great deal. Being raised under a Christian foundation has truly helped me to become the woman I am today. I thank God every day for my mother instilling that in her children from the very beginning of life.

Someone once told me I would never amount to anything because I had a baby at a young age. I believe life is not about what happens to you but, more about how you react to what happens to you. Being a single mother of three children at 23, working a full-time job, being in an abusive marriage, and going to school full time was not an easy task. There were many times I wanted to give up, but I can hear my pastor saying, "Where God guides, he provides." I'm a living witness to that. I pray about everything and embrace the Holy Spirit!

God ordered my steps to get out of the boat. You see, I believe some people come into your life for only for a season or a reason. Sometimes, it's until you realize you are still in the boat. You can look back over your life and understand it all if you are a child of God.

It took three marriages and the will of God for me to finally understand my purpose in life. You see, my ministry is giving back to the community and helping people better their lives through my experiences in life. Family hasn't always been there for me, and I've had to reach out to friends more than family. Life's challenges will have you in distress if you don't have God by your side. Now that I have my own family of 14 grandchildren and four great grandchildren from my three children, family is the most important thing to me; family gets me through those tough times. My siblings are my rock, and I pray I can depend on them when needed.

In the early 80s, I actually saw the light, but God was not ready for me. I was in intensive care for two weeks and had a 10% chance of surviving. God wants me to share my testimony with you! I had a massive stroke and never even knew it based upon what the doctor shared with me from the MRI of my brain. You see, I'm destined to fulfill God's purpose.

Growing up, I knew something was different about me from my siblings, but I could never pinpoint it. One day, riding in the car with my mother, she asked why I couldn't be more like my sister. I told her I was not my sister, and I was my own person, and the comment that I got back took my life in a spiral.

She said, "No, you're not like your sister because you have a different father."

I stopped the car and simply pulled over on the side of the road and said, "What!?"

I was 23 years old when I found out that the father that raised me was not my biological father. I was on a quest to find out who I really was. I needed to know my full background to help me understand myself. My mother only gave me a nickname, so I began my own research, and I found out my uncle knew the truth and how to contact my biological father. He arranged for me to talk to my father, even though my father did not know he had a daughter. He was married and pastored a church. After meeting my father, he said someone once told him he had a daughter in Florida but that was about it. My father was an ordained minister and had been for over 20 years. He and his wife accepted me with open arms and again I had plans to make up for lost time with my biological father. That was not God's plan. We loved each other until the day he passed away.

I learned I had four other siblings from my biological father, three from his first marriage, and an older brother from a previous relationship. I was able to bond with my older brother and we became the best of friends. He was 11 years older than me and lived about an hour away from where I lived. We were inseparable until he passed away. When I met my stepbrother, we fell in love and married but again that was not God's plan. We divorced and remained amicable until he passed away. My oldest brother from my mother's side of the family really looked up to me and he knew that there was nothing I couldn't do, and he admired me for that and told me often. We were best friends until he passed away. The brother that I grew up with from the father that raised me, which was two years older than me, we were inseparable as well. He was one of my husband's best friends. We would do things together all the time; if he wasn't visiting me, I was visiting him. He was my inspiration until he passed away.

I remember passing by a subdivision often commuting back and forth to work. I always looked at it and said I wanted to live there. I prayed about it frequently. We moved into the largest house in that subdivision. I thought I had it all: my perfect home. The house turned out to be a path for me to get to where God wanted me to be.

While working in the yard, my husband would often see a couple and they would give him business cards to come visit their church. And when walking the trail, I would meet another couple that always told me about their church. I had my eyes on joining another church. But again, that was my plan. It wasn't God's plan. God led us to the church from both couples' invitations and we found peace, love, protection, and the Holy Spirit; we became members.

Shortly after that, God spoke to me and told me to leave the home, sell or give away everything in the home, and leave it. I was obedient, and I did just that. You see, God had a plan for me, and it wasn't that house. That house was just another means for me to get closer to God. God was directing me to a place of worship. I have been a member of that church now for over 12 years. I was obedient to God and at the time I did not understand it, but I did it and we lived in an apartment for the next three years, but my God! My next home that I purchased came fully furnished; it was a beautiful home. So once again, where God guides, He provides. I had to be obedient to get the glory.

I met some beautiful God-fearing couples that led me to meeting other people and, once again, my plans were so different from God's plans. I was introduced to a group of women, and I was determined to fit in. The bonding was not effective for me, and I discontinued my relationship with the group. Once again, my plans differed from God's plans. One of my friends invited me to join a women's prayer group. After a few months, my friend quit the prayer group. I stayed on and was encouraged by, lo and behold, a woman I previously met through the group of women that I did not bond with. Once again, I can look back and clearly see God's plan. God's plan led me to the prayer group, and I have been participating for over four years now. Only God knew I truly needed the prayer group. I find it so exhilarating, beneficial, and godly, and it has helped me tremendously. The women are from all over the United States. We pray, share, and support each other.

Receiving God as my Lord and Savior and accepting that Jesus died for our sins has led me to do things that I never imagined—like overseeing finances for retreats, reading scriptures, and leading prayers. I am also active in my church. I've taught Sunday school, been the Master of Ceremony for church events, held financial literacy workshops, worked in the new members and visitor's ministry, and led the adult prayer warrior dance group. My ministry is giving back to the people what God has instilled within me through 42 years of financial experience, education, and a passion and will that come from the heart.

I was out of the boat a long time ago, but did not realize it until I allowed God to take control. If I can do it, so can you. Don't let life's challenges dictate your outcome. Give it to God. He will gladly take over if you allow Him— remember, He gives us free will. May God bless you continuously.

MEET THE AUTHOR | BRIDGET WELLS

Bridget is from upstate New York, but spent most of her childhood life traveling from the North to the South with her family as migrant workers. Bridget was the first of her family to graduate from college despite challenges growing up in a male dominant industry. Bridget holds a BS in Business Administration from Bethune Cookman University and a Master's in Organizational Management from the University of Phoenix.

Bridget has worked in the financial arena for 42 years. She exemplifies a passion for helping people from providing credit seminars at her church, mentoring high schoolers, serving on the Board of Directors for American Talent Development, etc. For over five years, she has been fulfilling her dream with Operation HOPE counseling clients on credit, money management, and homeownership.

Bridget became a born-again Christian many decades ago. She enjoys spending time with her three children, fourteen grandchildren, four great grandchildren, and other family and friends.

JOURNEY TO FREEDOM
CAROLYN R. INMAN

In the Bible, Hebrew Chapter 11:1 states, *"**Now faith is the substance of things hoped for, the evidence of things not seen.**"* For me, this means my past was a trampoline for my future. My faith is anchored in the Word of God, and I am rooted and anchored in faith. In my early years, I was often sent to South Carolina with my grandmother. This shaped me and sheltered me from the city life—but it also left me a bit naïve. In my early years, I was made to feel like I had to measure up to someone else's life—without truly knowing my own. It wasn't until my teenage years, graduating from high school, and going to college that I began to discover who I was. That's when the real drama of life began.

I enlisted in the Air Force and married in the Philippines, which I was one of the first black sergeants that was approved by letter from the Pentagon to stay in the military while pregnant. I later gave birth to my son,

Chester, at Mathers Air Force Base in Sacramento, CA in November 1972. That's where my relationship with God truly started—with my son. I asked for a son, and God blessed me with Chester. I feel my life really started then. That's when I started looking at my glass as being half full instead of empty. That's when I realized the importance of having a God in my life to get me through what I was going through.

I've done the best I could for the people I love—family and friends—often expecting more than I received. Those expectations, though sometimes unrealistic, caused me pain. At this point in my life, I'm searching for happiness, companionship, and love. I know I carry happiness and love within myself, but I still struggle with companionship and accepting my appearance at times. I'm working on that.

After taking a hard look at what's been keeping me depressed, I've realized—it's my past. As a child, certain ideas were planted in my mind, and I held onto the negative, never really seeing the positive. But I'm learning to let the past go. Yes, it shaped me and even made me stronger, but there are parts I no longer want to carry into my present.

The holidays are especially difficult. They bring up feelings of loneliness and sadness. There's no joy or celebration around me, and I feel deeply alone.

Recently, I reflected on the reasons behind my depression and what I could actually change. One of those reflections involved Chester. He used to ask why I get so down during the holidays. This time, I was honest with him—I told him about the lack of festivities, the loss of loved ones, the shift in my finances over time, and how my illnesses have changed me.

My new beginnings were frightful. Facing my truths, I realize I have less time ahead of me than behind me—and I want to enjoy what's left.

My new beginnings started 3 ½ years ago when I was invited to a prayer line by a friend, whom I also call my sister, Brenda Simpson. She has been a part of my life for 52 years. Brenda knew I was broken—by sexual trauma, bad marriages, medical issues, and life's many challenges.

I am a recovering addict, with 33 years of sobriety, and I've learned how to live through the tools of a 12-step program. Another life-changing tool was the introduction to the prayer warriors on the prayer line. They began praying for me, my son, my grandson, and our family struggles.

I started praying every day with the Serenity Prayer, and after two years of meeting every Sunday on the prayer line, my journey of healing truly took root.

Other spiritual realms—and the warrior women in my life—prayed over me and helped carry me through. They supported me through my family's drama, the weight that was unfairly placed on me. There was a time when I believed I wasn't a good mother or grandmother. But only God—His love and His wisdom—showed me otherwise.

My initial understanding of life came from my grandmother. *Can you hear me?* She helped me understand that God loves everyone, no matter their shade of skin. I love her deeply for instilling that in me. For years, I struggled with low self-esteem because of my complexion.

But as I began living my adult life—and gaining a deeper understanding of the God I serve—I also began to love myself. That's when everything started to change.

I stopped feeling like I was *less than* or *not enough*. I began to acknowledge what I *had* achieved rather than focusing on what I hadn't. I started to see my cup as full—not empty. I began to look in the mirror and see a beautiful, God-given woman, regardless of my medical issues.

I thank God and am truly grateful for all He has allowed me to do.

This is my story.

This is my journey.

And now?

I am out of the boat of bondage and free. Thank God.

The life I live today is centered around God. I live a peaceful, stress-free life. I wake up each day thanking God for another chance, and I always say a little prayer I'd love to share with you:

I want your life to be a wonderful one. I wish you peace deep within your soul, joyfulness, and the promise of each new day.

May you reach for your dreams, create memories more beautiful than words can say, and understand how special you truly are. May your journey be safe from storms and warmed by the sun—a path to wonderful things, an invitation to the abundance life brings, and an angel watching over you for all the days to come. May you find the path on your journey that will lead you to getting out of the boat!

MEET THE AUTHOR | CAROLYN R. INMAN

Carolyn R. Inman was born and raised in Philadelphia, Pennsylvania, the youngest of three siblings—one brother and one sister—born to loving and caring parents, Calvin Lee and Ruberta Iman.

She enjoyed school from an early age and was raised in the church, where she was baptized at the age of six. In her youth, she ran track, played the piano, and took ballet lessons.

After graduating from high school, Carolyn attended college and later joined the United States Air Force, where she served honorably. Following her military service, she was employed by Pacific Telephone Company and eventually transferred to Bell Atlantic, from which she retired after a successful career.

She is a member of Mount Airy Church of God in Christ, under the leadership of Dr. Felton, where she has faithfully served as an usher for the past three years.

She enjoys spending time with her family, serving God, and living life to the fullest.

Carolyn proudly dedicates this book to her son, Chester Calvin Lee Talbert, and her grandson, Dache Lee Talbert. As a single mother to her son and a strong support system for her grandson, she is incredibly proud of both.

MOVE FROM FAITH TO FAITH
DEBRA COFER

It is important to keep the faith and trust God as you walk out the journey and purpose He has planned for your life. When I reflect on the journey God has for my life, I realize how incredible my journey has been so far and God's master plan through it all.

It began in Orlando, FL—I'm a proud Florida native. One of my favorite supervisors chose me to go with her to Atlanta to help with the workload because they were backed up. We flew to Atlanta for two weeks to help. When we got back to our Orlando office, we found out the other clerks had filed a grievance against her because they had more seniority than I did. They won the grievance.

Nevertheless, it was truly a blessing that I went. As it turns out, the same place I went to help in Atlanta was the same location but different area, where I would start my new job just six months later. It was a part of God's plan for me to move to Atlanta. I had no family there, but I had stepped out on faith and applied for the position in Atlanta. Two months later, the transfer went through. I got the job and accepted the position. I was excited and scared, but didn't let that stop me.

The Sunday before moving to Atlanta, I went to church at Shiloh Missionary Baptist Church, where I was a member. Before benediction, they asked if anybody wanted prayer —so I went up front for prayer. I also talked to the pastor to let him know I was moving. The pastor said, "If you believe this is God's will for you, do it. Keep the faith and it will work out."

I had four requests of God, and he answered every one. I asked not to live far from my job, to be able to go home to visit my mom when I wanted to, for the job to work out, and to find a church home.

My friend, Pat, welcomed me into her home for almost four years. It was only about 20 minutes away from the job. I was so happy it was not far at all, but I was missing my family and friends in Orlando. One evening my friend Georgia, who lived in Orlando, called me and said she was mailing me a letter because God woke her up at 5:30am to write this letter to me. She instructed me to read it the next time I was feeling down and having doubts about my decision to move to Atlanta.

That day came when I knew I was supposed to read this letter. I had job concerns, and I had visited several churches but had not found a church home yet. This is what the letter said:

December 22nd, 1995.

My dearest Debra, I am sure you thought it to be strange for me to want to write you a letter; but there is nothing strange about wanting your sister in the spirit to be happy in the Lord in spirit, truth, and strength. As I began it is 5:30am (my best time, not yours, right?) God loves you and I love you, for you are lovable, kind, and sincere. Always remember that, Debra. God will have you live your life in confidence of His promises and his word. For His word never changes. He is Alpha and Omega, the First and the Last, the beginning and the end, says the Lord, who is and who was and who is to come—the almighty (Revelation 1:18). You have made a wise choice to move from familiar to unfamiliar, from the old to the new, from comfort to a walk of faith that some would not have the courage or faith to take, so be strong (2 Timothy 1:1). Be strong in the grace that is in Christ Jesus. You will have days of total happiness and bliss —peaks and valleys, but continue to bless the Lord at all times and allow praise to continually be in your mouth (Psalm 34:1). If you have struggles, this is good. You are strong in your faith. Ask Jesus to be your intercessor and pray for help (Psalm 35). Plead my case, Lord, with those who strive with me and fight against those who fight against me. In all you do, you must put your trust in God. You will be in a new situation, your new home, and your new job. You must remember there is growth— spiritual—in change. You have chosen to walk a walk of faith, so be alert. If there is confusion, you know God is not the author of confusion; God is a God of decency and order. (Corinthians 14:40) If you need a sign, He will give you one. If you want confirmation, He will give you one. He will supply all your needs. If you need me, call me. If not, call occasionally anyway.

Spiritually growing sisters, with your degree of willingness and sincerity to grow strong in the world, are like rare jewels. I love you Debra and I will be praying for you always.

When I read her letter, it was exactly what I needed. It lifted my spirits and encouraged me to keep going and reassured me that God had my back. This letter from Georgia had a significant impact on my life and spurred my ability to continue moving from faith to faith, getting out of the boat, and trusting God. I will always remember Georgia—may she rest in peace.

Before starting the six-week training for my new job, I heard rumors NYPS was a difficult and stressful job, so I called my sister. She said, "You will do fine because you are going to be trained for the job. Just ask questions in training if there's anything you don't understand," reassuring me I was more than capable of doing it. I took my sister's advice and training went well and I really liked my job.

Some ladies on my job and I remembered each other from my previous visit to Atlanta. One of them was a member of New Birth Missionary Baptist Church - Decatur, Ga under the leadership of Bishop Eddie L. Long, and she invited me to visit. Several other people also mentioned New Birth, so I visited. The first time I visited New Birth, I knew it was the church home where God wanted me to be. I took several classes. I was in the women's choir and attended Wednesday Bible study and Sunday morning service. My spiritual growth deepened, my relationship with God became closer, and my faith grew even stronger.

Next, it was time to move out of Pat's home to see what God had for me next. After I moved out, I called Pat and let her know I appreciated her letting me stay with her. She replied, "I would do it all over again."

Soon afterward, God blessed me with a loving, supportive husband, Dennis Cofer, and our lovely extended family. After 10 years, we downsized and bought a house in College Park, Ga. We had also bought a house in Orlando. Because of the move, we left New Birth, and now attended Impact Church.

I had retired after 30 years at AT&T NYPS department and had to find something new I would enjoy doing. I fed the community at the church in downtown Atlanta, line danced at Beulah Life Center, and did Zumba at L Claudia Allen Center in Orlando.

It was our goal to help take care of our parents because they were getting older and we wanted to spend more time with them, but before it materialized my husband's mom passed and then my mom passed six months later. This was such a tough time for us to deal with losing our moms. It was a tough decision, but we went forward with having dual homes. We would go back and forth every three months.

At my Zumba class, I met new friends; we formed the retired ladies' group called *Sistas Rock*. It was six of us. We did different activities and had fun outings. I was the coordinator for the events, and it lasted for seven years.

My husband grew tired of driving back and forth from Orlando to Atlanta. It had been 12 years. The housing market was good. The opportunity came for us to sell the house in College Park, Ga. So, we put the house up for sale. The first and second deal fell through, and the third deal was the blessing. The lady, Jessica, had received an inheritance from her grandma, and she bought our house with cash. We got to meet her at closing, and she said that she loved the house. She shared with us that she had put in an offer to buy a condo, and when she went to do the walkthrough of the condo, sheetrock from the second floor had fallen to the first floor because of a burst water pipe. She backed up out of there and left. Her cousin had told her about our house and so she came by to look at it and contacted our realtor. The realtor called us while we were in Orlando, so we had to rush back to Atlanta for closing.

Now it was time to pack, and Tina helped me pack. That morning, I told her whatever she saw in the house and wanted, she could have. She was overjoyed and had tears in her eyes. She was a single mother with three kids and needed to furnish her place. After finishing packing, I asked Tina how much I owed her for her help, and she said nothing. She said God put it on her heart not to charge me anything. But God led me to bless her monetarily. She was a godsend. The moving went smoother than I expected.

Everything was going well and then in 2019, everything changed. Because of COVID, I was no longer going to various places. I missed going to church and feeding the community on Tuesday. I prayed about it, and I realized how important it is for believers to come together in prayer, so I started a prayer line in November 2020.

It was becoming overwhelming to do both the prayer line and Sistas Rock. At the beginning of the year, *Sistas Rock* had a meeting over the phone, and I let them know I could not coordinate events for *Sistas Rock* anymore. God was preparing and positioning me as the hostess for the prayer line. The prayer line was going well. People came and left, but God always brought new people on the prayer call that were committed and dedicated to the vision He had given me. It continued to flourish and grow. We started with 18 people and now we have over 40 people on the prayer call.

The first anniversary for the prayer line, we did a zoom call so now we could put faces with the names. It went very well, so the next year God laid it on my heart to do a retreat. It all came together. I looked for an Airbnb, and almost gave up, but I called Top Villas, and I got the right person. She said she was a Christian, and that she would help me even if she had to come in early and stay late to find the right place for us, and she did. She gave us a discount and said admired what we were doing. It was 28 ladies there, 20 stayed overnight, 8 came over in the daytime. We had a wonderful time; it was successful. It was great fellowship, fun, and delicious food—including a chef for Saturday's brunch and dinner. The villa accommodated us perfectly. We were there from Friday night at 6:00pm until Monday morning at 9:00am. God blessed it from the start to the end. I called the lady at Top

Villas to thank her, but she no longer worked there, so God allowed her to be there at that time to find the right villa for us. I wanted to make sure it was reasonably affordable for each person to attend. God laid it on my heart to sow a seed toward the retreat, and I did. God blessed me to receive even more than I sowed. Keep the faith and be led by God and He will bless you.

I want to thank God for my loving husband being supportive and being there for me, and I want to thank my sister and a couple of my friends from Atlanta for helping me in the background. I thank God for every person who helped me with the retreat. I could not have done it without them. The theme for the retreat was *Get out of the Boat*. My friend, Vera, was the speaker God had to bring the message. It was a powerful message. It blessed me. This is when I really experienced and understood what it meant to get out of the boat—stepping out of my comfort zone, being led by God, and recognizing how far He has brought me. It was a season of change and deep spiritual growth.

As I look back at what God has done, I now look forward with excitement and expectation for what He has in store for the prayer line and my life. By keeping the faith, I am continually reminded of what getting out of the boat looks like, time and time again. I trust God because He is the Author of my life. It is this trust that gives us the courage to get out of the boat!

Meet the Author | Debra Cofer

Debra Cofer is the founder and hostess of the prayer line —a vision divinely given to her by God. Every Sunday, she gathers with a group of women brought together by faith and purpose. They pray together, lift each other up, and intercede for others, experiencing the power of iron sharpening iron in every call.

After graduating from high school, Debra attended Valencia Community College before beginning her career at Southern Bell. She started in Orlando, later transferring to Atlanta, and eventually retired after 30 years of service with AT&T as a National Account Coordinator. She has now been enjoying retirement for 13 years.

Debra has always had a heart for service. She served as a Junior Woman and usher at Shiloh Missionary Baptist Church, sang in the choir, and took spiritual development classes at New Birth. She also helped feed the community through Hugs Ministries.

With a passion for helping and fellowshipping with others, Debra continues to live a purpose-filled life. In her spare time, she enjoys working out and playing sports—and above all, she remains committed to doing what God has called her to do. It has truly been a blessing.

Debra is family oriented and loves nothing more than spending time with her family. She has been blessed with a loving and supportive husband, Dennis Cofer, wonderful bonus children, and three grandchildren that are loved and adored.

WORKING OUT MY PURPOSE
GLENDA D. RICHARDSON

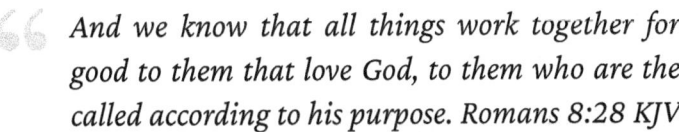 *And we know that all things work together for good to them that love God, to them who are the called according to his purpose. Romans 8:28 KJV*

I will bless the Lord at all times and his praise shall continually be in my mouth. My soul shall boast in the lord and be glad, oh magnify the Lord with me and let us exalt his name together. Psalms 34:1

I t all began over thirty years ago, a very good friend, and I started a "Prayer Chain" group by phone. It included individuals from various church denominations, young and older saints, who participated in this evolving effort. This was established based on our desire to see changes occur in our lives. Even though we attended church regularly with our families and friends, it became boring and unfulfilling. Therefore, we realized that there's more to our faith than just attending worship services, Sunday school, and other related church activities—so we did something different and challenging.

During this time, I was so devastated and emotionally hurt and felt like giving up. I had experienced the loss of my sister and later came the death of my father. I carried my problems within because I didn't feel comfortable sharing my concerns with others. A trust issue was rising within me that I kept to myself, and I wasn't sure how to express those feelings to my family members. It never occurred to me how deeply I was hurting on the inside. At this point in my life, I believed I was a born-again (saved) believer, but it felt like I just couldn't get it together or move forward.

As I continued to attend church and hear preached messages and read my bible, things changed for me. I experienced the baptism of the Holy Spirit one Sunday evening at my church. This experience was so amazing and overwhelming for me that it confirmed for me—without a doubt—that God is real and more than I can imagine. From that moment, spiritual growth took over, and I became hungry for more of Him. Now, I find myself asking, *"Where do I go from this point on? What's next?"*

Well, as we talked it over again, we decided we must do something we've never done before and that was to pray to God about our situations and believe He would answer.

The Holy Spirit had birthed in me a desire to start a prayer chain, which included five to seven people on the call. We began prayer at 6:00am every morning before work for five days a week. I asked a co-worker if he would create a prayer board chart for requests to include names, dates, and times of when God answered our prayers. We collected and recorded all the individuals' information and prayed corporately over their personal requests and believe God that he would answer us.

Jeremiah 33:3 says, *"Call unto me, and I will answer thee, and shew thee great and mighty things, which thou knowest not."* Remarkably, we stepped out in our faith to believe that God's word is true, alive, and active! Knowing that his promises are yes and amen!

Hebrews 4:12 states: *"For the word of God is quick, and powerful and sharper than a two-edged sword piercing even to the dividing asunder of soul and spirit, and of the joints and marrow, and is a discerner of the thoughts and intents of the heart."*

As a prayer group, we purchased a book entitled, "What Happens When Women Pray," by Evelyn Christensen. This was part of the beginning of the shift for me. I was so excited! This book encouraged the group in so many ways whereby it equipped, enhanced, and developed our lives to change spiritually. This book eventually challenged me to become a strong prayer warrior by memorizing scriptures and incorporating them into my prayer life daily. When I became serious about my relationship with God, things changed—how I talked, where I went, who I connected with, and my decision making. This allowed me to see how the word of God keeps us focused on watching our words and how it can affect our lifestyles as believers. Remember, there is power in your words. There is life or death spoken from your mouth; so be careful of what you say.

Throughout these prayer sessions, there were many testimonies shared among each other as we discussed diverse topics. Let us reflect on a few testimonies. Because of our time, commitment, and faithfulness in prayer. I recalled about a year into the prayer circle, a friend's mom accepted Jesus as her Savior and Lord. Then later, about a couple of years, her father committed his life to God, and he never turned back. PRAISE GOD! HALLELUJAH! This is what happens when women pray.

Another prayer request was for a mother's son—healing in his brain and salvation for her husband. We were elated for her, witnessing the power of God being manifested. In fact, her son is still living to this day, but the parents are both deceased now.

There were at least eight to twelve ladies in attendance. Some were ministers, evangelists, and teachers who participated. These individuals were from different church affiliations; however, it did not matter because we all had one purpose in mind—to pray and see the manifestation of our prayers.

As we continued in our prayer group, which was held at my home in Orlando, FL, we would gather in prayer for peace in our community, crime, family, jobs, and relationships. We even prayed for individuals outside of the group as well.

The prayer list grew enormously, and we were eager to trust God and acknowledge His presence during our sessions. The move of God was so amazing and powerful to many, and we rejoiced in every moment. The word of God declares in 1 Thessalonians 5:16-18, *"Rejoice evermore. Pray without ceasing. In everything give thanks: for this is the will of God in Christ Jesus concerning you."* (KJV)

Now let us focus on the *heart* of a man or woman. In the book of Proverbs 3:5-7 states, *"Trust in the Lord with all thine **heart**; and lean not unto thine own understanding. In all thy ways acknowledge him and he shall direct thy paths. Be not wise in thine own eyes; **fear** the Lord and depart from evil."*

The word heart is a noun defined as "the organ which functions in the human body to keep us alive." However, this passage refers to an individual's physical, emotional, and moral intent of the heart, mind, body, and soul. When I received the understanding of this scripture, my faith was enlightened and elevated spiritually in seeing the manifestation of all answered prayers.

In the bible, according to Hebrew 11:1; *"now faith is the substance of things hoped for the evidence of things not seen."* And Hebrew 11:3 says, *"Through faith, we understand the word of God framed the worlds, so that things which are seen were not made of things which do appear."*

As we journeyed through this time, we learned the process of believing, trusting, hoping, and declaring the goodness of God's grace and mercy, which kept us motivated in this project. Because of our commitment and dedication, it has been proven that when we commit our life in prayer, our relationship is strengthened in God. Therefore, being a prayer warrior increased our faith and hunger to commit to a life of righteousness. Because of our consistent prayer life, many have developed spiritual leadership qualities birthed through the Holy Spirit, such as intercessors, teachers, evangelists, pastors, and ministers. We have a responsibility as believers in Christ to share our experiences within our church and community to ignite hope in the lives of all people.

Finally, there are spiritual materials you will need to maintain a personal and effective prayer life.

1. **A good study Bible.** This will enhance your spiritual growth through your faith and belief system. I would recommend the MacArthur, Scoffield, and Life Application Study Bible.
2. **A Bible Dictionary**
3. Be selective in choosing **spiritual materials** for your personal study and as a guide for your spiritual growth.
4. **A journal.** This is where you will record your dreams and visions from God. In doing this, the Holy Spirit will guide you in the will of God for your life.
5. **Concordance.** A cross-reference guide for seeking scriptures as it relates to any subject.
6. **Daily Meditation and study** of the word.
7. **Discipline and commitment to prayer.**
8. **A Prayer Visual Board**

9. **A Prayer Room** in your home where it is conducive for a quiet setting with few distractions. Have the atmosphere accommodated with worship music, pictures which depict the sound of worship, along with colorful images. This will be your place of meeting with your Heavenly Father in pouring out your problems.
10. **Consistency.** Establish a **prayer time** in the morning before starting your day. Keep it going throughout the day at noon or whenever you have a lunch break from work. Stay focused on that time spent and do not exceed it. That is so vital. Always close your day with prayer, asking for God's covering and divine protection.
11. **An Accountability Partne**r. A person who is dedicated to prayer and has a desire to commit to it. He or she will sacrifice their time and energy, spiritually growing along with you.

Remember, as you begin your journey in "stepping out of the boat" in prayer, allow the Holy Spirit to lead you—building your self-esteem and confidence as you pursue your destiny and trust the process to walk fully in the mantle God has purposed for you.

MEET THE AUTHOR | GLENDA D. RICHARDSON

Born and raised in Orlando, Florida, Glenda Richardson embarked on a journey marked by both personal and professional accomplishments. After graduating in 1977, she pursued higher education with determination, earning a bachelor's degree in Business Administration from Columbia College University. This strong academic foundation paved the way for a fulfilling career that blended her passion for education with her commitment to service.

Glenda later earned a master's degree in Special Education from Grand Canyon University. With a heart for teaching, she spent 15 years in the education system, positively impacting countless students. She also dedicated time to tutoring young, school-aged children, providing personalized support and mentorship to help them thrive.

In 2020, life presented Glenda with a new challenge when she became disabled. Yet, she remained committed to a life of service and purpose. As a Licensed Minister and Elder at Warriors of Christ Ministry, Glenda continues to provide spiritual guidance and support within her community. Her heart for service also extends to volunteering at senior facilities, nursing homes, and other local organizations, offering comfort and building meaningful relationships.

Family plays a central role in Glenda's life. She has been married to her husband, Michael, for 12 years, and together they have two children, Chris and Joie, and two grandchildren, Avery and Allie. Their love and strong family bond remain a source of strength and joy.

Now residing in Wilmington, North Carolina, Glenda enjoys traveling, reading, exploring nature, listening to music, appreciating the arts, and indulging in a little shopping—all of which bring balance and inspiration to her life.

Through all of life's changes and challenges, Glenda Richardson remains steadfast in her mission to live with purpose, serve others, and cherish the blessings of faith, family, and community.

Scripture: *"And the Lord answered me, and said, Write the vision, and make it plain upon tables, that he may run that readeth it."* —Habakkuk 2:2

Purpose: Glenda Richardson's purpose is to encourage

readers by sharing how she built and continues to foster a deep relationship with God through intercessory prayer.

Hymn: "Sweet Hour of Prayer" is a very familiar hymn that was sung in the African American churches which lingers in our hearts so richly today and gives us a great warm sensation of relief. It was sung during prayer meetings, bible study, and church revivals.

HE WILL NEVER LEAVE YOU
LINDA DENMARK-AUSTIN

I am the oldest of six children. Ever sense I can remember, I was always different, always believed that there is a God—so much so that I was baptized five times as a child. Until my grandmother explained to me: you only have to be baptized once. I always wanted to know more about God—how He works and more about His signs, miracles, and wonders. Everyone has seasons in their life where we try to validate our worth, not knowing that we are precious gems in His sight. God has a plan for all of us.

There was a period in my life that I wondered who or if anyone cared for me. And then there was Jesus. (1 Peter 5:7) I went to this little, one room building church where everyone—men, women, and children—were all dressed in white from head to toe on a Wednesday evening. There were saints laying hands and praying for me to receive salvation in the name of the Father (God), the Son (Jesus) and the Holy Spirit (Holy Ghost). Thinking and not knowing what to expect—just wanting everything to be alright and for someone to care. Hoping the pain was over, not realizing it had only just begun. This life comes with a price to pay—eternal life in Christ Jesus (although Jesus has already paid the price). I had forgotten what my grandmother would always tell me as a child. She would sing a song called *"Jesus Loves Me"* and remind me that one day on Calvary, He died for me. That even as I was being formed in my mother's womb, He knew that this day was coming. That wanting to know more about Him, there would come a time in my life when I would feel compelled to stop doing certain things like smoking cigarettes, go clubbing, and dating married men. At that point, God began giving me favor with wisdom and knowledge to understand that I was no longer my own, but now I have been bought with a price (1 Corinthian 6:19). I actually went to this church to find out why my brother no longer celebrated Christmas or gave gifts. We were raised in a household that believed December 25th was Christmas Day, and we always exchanged gifts. Little did I know, that visit would lead to a major change in my life.

The more I went to the church, the more I wanted to be there. I went from one day at church and one day for bible study, to now attending seven days a week. Something new was occurring. The table had been spread, and each time I sat at the table it was like I had a personal invitation from God to receive another nugget of wisdom (1 Corinthians 5:17). I was so inspired that I even began having bible studies in my van with two other people during my lunch break at work.

Challenges arose when a colleague once asked me, "Why do you always thank God? You can do things yourself." This was the same colleague who often used racial slurs in the office. Still, I continued to give thanks to God.

One day, she asked why people say the Lord's Prayer and what it means. From there, she began asking more questions about the Word of God—every day. Eventually, she said she wanted to be baptized.

It got to the point where we couldn't even tell who was saying "Thank you, Jesus" more! As 1 Thessalonians 5:18 reminds us, *"Give thanks in all circumstances..."*—and God gave me favor.

She invited me to her wedding and to witness her baptism. Now, 37 years later, we are still sisters in Christ.

God is a compass in our life's journey—working in all directions and leading and guiding us south, north, east and west. Yet, through it all, He remains the center point. The company gave us employees four vans to carpool. Our van traveled from the east. It was special. There were six members aboard who all showed compassion towards one another's needs—whether it was stopping to pick up medicine, arranging childcare, or giving someone a ride if they were having car problems. We always prayed before pulling off in the morning and evening, and God showed us many things while riding in the van. He helped us to understand and pray more for each other. The other three vans were not reinstated. People just could not show love toward one another. Remember, God does not work in mess (1 Corinthians 14:33).

We kept our van over 15 years. At that time, gas was at an all-time high. Most of the ladies in this van were single parents, and we only paid $10 a week. God will make a way out of no way. God will provide. (Philippians 4:19) God says it is alright to ask Him for what you need. Some ladies got married, some divorced, some became entrepreneurs, and others became leaders in their church. There was a time I found myself in trouble, but God proved to me He is a present help in the time of trouble. (Psalm 46:1). Our journeys are different, but yet the same. That is why we had a team of peoples to help each other.

Once that seed is planted—to help or nurture—there is a hunger to feed and share with others the word of God. Just as little children, we become sponges wanting to know and do new things that are in God. The more we give of ourselves, the more He will give of Himself.

Working outside of the church walls helped me grow and find out who I really am. It taught me a lot about myself —meeting all types of people, some with more knowledge of the bible than me. I began doing homeless street ministry and meeting lots of people—some just doing their own thing and others hungry to know that God cares for us. (1Peter 5:7) There are players on each of our shoulders—the good player and the evil player—the question is who you will follow.

The church team took a trip to a bridge under Edgewood Ave where a colony of homeless people reside with different needs: clothes, food, and prayer. Once I met a man with throat cancer and other health issues who had been there for 10 years. Each week, we prayed with him and fed him natural food and the word of God. One evening, he decided he wanted to come to church and arrangements were made for his pickup so he could get there. By him being open to hear the word of God, God worked on his behalf by supplying him with a home—which meant that he was no longer living under the bridge. Now he has a car, social security, and became a deacon in the church. Glory to God for the things He can, will and has done. As I think back over my life, I know it was nobody but God that kept me even before I had known Him for myself.

I was the same young lady with a bad attitude and who was pronounced dead at the scene of a serious vehicle accident. But my grandmother had always taught me to pray even if it is a short prayer like *"Lord, have mercy."* I saw the light, asked God to forgive me, and promised to change my ways. While in the hospital, I went looking for the lady that was in the other vehicle. We had sustained the same injuries, but her injuries were more severe. She greeted me with a smile, thanked me for finding her, and apologized for the accident her husband caused with his confused mind. I knew then something had happened to me. When you have a true encounter with God, you are never the same again. No matter how hard you try to fit in with the world, even they can tell that you are different.

God left a few scars to remind me of the promise between Him and me—another day's journey, covered by new mercies and grace.

But this was the hardest part: I expected to see, yet my natural eyesight was failing me daily. It felt like I was going blind. I thought I was losing my mind. Everything was slipping away—mentally and physically. My old flesh kicked in, and that pity spirit took over.

All I wanted was to lie in bed and cry—day and night. I isolated myself from others. I couldn't eat, sleep, or pray. My mind was blank. I couldn't concentrate or even remember what I had done just a minute earlier.

It seemed like everything was slipping away.

And then suddenly, the telephone rang—a prayer warrior was on the other end, saying that God had placed me on her heart. I asked her to pray for me.

Before I go any further, I have to say: God is faithful *(Psalm 57:3–11)*. Even then, I still didn't feel completely like myself.

The only scriptures I could remember were *The Lord's Prayer (Matthew 6:9–13)* and *The Lord is My Shepherd (Psalm 23)*—and even then, I could only recall parts of them.

But I do remember calling on the name of Jesus over and over—*Jesus, Jesus, Jesus (Acts 4:12)*—pleading, "Help me, Lord, break these chains that are holding me back from You."

The next morning, I heard the Holy Ghost say, "Get up. Go wash your face in cold water." From that moment, I felt a change in my emotions. The sadness was not as strong as before. I was no longer fatigued or having brain fog. I was beginning to feel like myself again, thanking and praising God for all that He does (John 14:13-14).

As a Christian; I have the tendency to be a caregiver most times—putting others' needs before my own. Sometimes God will sit you down so that you can hear Him (Psalms 46:0). We live in a microwave world. Everything is now! Fast! This causes stress. After resting and talking with God, I felt sober-minded and at peace once again. I went about my daily tasks knowing that God holds all my beginnings and endings in His hands. That there is no one like Him and that He is true to His word. He will never leave us or forsake us.

For example, once a tree fell on my house. It was lying on the edge against the roof and gutters. I did not know what to do, so I pulled from my childhood lessons and said what I was taught, "Lord, have mercy." Then I left and went to the store. When I returned home, someone had cut up and removed the tree. All that remained was a bent gutter. Even until today, I do not know who removed that tree. I asked the neighbors. No one saw the person who showed such a kind act of love (John 13:34-35).

All we have to do is call Him and He will answer (Matt 7:7-8). All blessings come from God, regardless of how they come.

MEET THE AUTHOR | LINDA DENMARK-AUSTIN

Linda Denmark-Austin, mother of two and grandmother of five, shares these inspirational memories of her grandparents, James and Julia—the first to tell her about God. Growing up in their home meant waking up to gospel music and a hot breakfast, and ending each day on your knees in prayer before being tucked in. She hopes these small nuggets of inspiration will enlighten your heart and remind you that Jesus loves you—and He will never forsake you.

ANCHOR OF FAITH
OLLIE L. LOFTON

I never learned to swim. My Father died when I was 14 months old. I'm not quite sure of the timing, it could have been on his deathbed, but my mother and grandmother told my two brothers, sister, and I my father said to keep us away from the water because one of us would drown. I guess you can say he'd had a premonition. So, I never learned to swim. Nevertheless, I've always been drawn to the water. The sound of the waves crashing into one another, the smell of the ocean, the reflection of the moonlight on the water, has always been alluring to me.

The first time I was in a boat, I took a ride down the Intercoastal Waterway. The owner and captain of the boat was experienced, so I was able to let my hair down and enjoy the moment as we sped down the coast from Delray Beach up to West Palm Beach and then back to Delray. On the ride to West Palm Beach, I suddenly became fearful as the memory of my father's premonition crossed my mind. Then panic crept in! Oh goodness! What was I doing in a boat? Had I completely lost my mind? Was I the one my father dreamt had drowned? How had I let anyone talk me into getting into a boat? And more importantly...how had I let anyone talk me into taking my 2-yr old daughter along for the ride? Sure, we had on life jackets, but I CAN'T SWIM! How was I going to save my daughter if anything happened? Sure, the water was beautiful; the boat appeared to be riding the waves with ease and the wind was blowing in my hair, but I NEVER LEARNED TO SWIM! When we finally reached West Palm Beach, the captain slowed the speed, and we headed back, but before we did, he wanted to take us for a brief excursion into the ocean. Now I knew geography and had received good grades in school, so I knew what body of water was on the east coast of Florida. Surely, he couldn't be talking about the Atlantic Ocean—the second largest ocean in the world! As I said, "No," I could see the color of the water changing and I knew we were already at the edge of the Atlantic Ocean! A few minutes later, the captain slowed the speed of the boat again and made a wide turn. I knew then that we were heading back to the Intercoastal Waterway. On the ride back, I finally relaxed and enjoyed the ride. I remember holding my daughter close and then closing my eyes, simply feeling the wind on my face and through my hair. I felt calm and peaceful. I was living in the moment, and I did not want the moment to end. Why the sudden change? I realized it was because I trusted the captain with my life and the precious life of my daughter. He was the owner of the boat, and I knew he could steer the boat as he had done dozens of times before.

Why did I choose to tell this story? There are several reasons. As I wrote about getting out of the boat, I realized I first had to get into the boat before I could get out of it. If I was going to conquer my fear of the water, I needed to be in it rather than watching safely from the shoreline. Certainly, if a huge wave came towards the shoreline, I would see it in time to move back to a safe zone. No harm, no foul, right? Most times, I think we do ourselves an injustice because we are afraid of failing. Afraid failure would show others we may not be as strong, capable, or resilient as we portray ourselves daily.

The other reason I reminisced about the boat experience is because, after all these years, the memory was still vivid in my mind, even though it was some 40-odd years ago. The experience was a combination of sweet and salty, calm and windy all at the same time. It reminded me of so many other situations and circumstances I've experienced as I grew older and journeyed through life. Some of my greatest joys have come from letting go of fear and doubt; learning to trust my own instincts and trusting foremost that God's word will not come back null or void. For His word says in Hebrews 13:5, *I will neither leave you nor forsake thee.*

So often in life we put our faith in people, places, and things that we 100% believe in. For some reason, it's easy to convince us of the things we have strong convictions about. And yet, for many reasons, we often find it hard to have faith in the Word. For example, we go to restaurants, and we believe the chef is using the freshest vegetables, the best ingredients, and the server has the highest standard of cleanliness. The food before us will look amazing and will be so satisfying to our palettes. We anticipate thoroughly enjoying the meal and being able to call it a good day. We never think that the food on the plate will look unattractive, nor will it make us ill. And yet we do not know the chef or server or whether either of them has had a horrible day. We may even forget to pray over the food once it is served. And yet we trust the process. Another example, when we board a flight, we trust the flight attendants will be friendly; the pilots experienced, and, if flying alone; the people seated next to us are just as kind and thoughtful as we are. We also trust the flight will be without incident and will arrive safely at our destination. The vacation will be filled with wonderful memories that will last a lifetime. Afterwards, we'll head back to the airport and fall asleep on the flight home. Again, we trust the process.

I got on that boat all those years ago, fully knowing that I could not swim, nor had I ever been close to that much water in my lifetime. I trusted the captain, and I also wanted to impress him and be fearless. So why do we question God and not trust in His word? Why do we worry and pray at the same time? Time after time, God protects us from others as well as ourselves. Danger seems to lurk on every corner, and we should not hesitate to suit up and put on the whole armor of God as described in Ephesians chapter 6.

When Debra, the host of the Prayer Warriors group, first sent me the invitation to join the weekly calls in 2020, the time of the pandemic, I joined the calls sporadically. I traveled back and forth with my daughter almost every weekend to help take care of my mom, who passed October 2024 at the seasoned age of 101. I'm so grateful for the number of years God allowed her to be here with us on this side of the river. But that's another story for another day. As for the Prayer Warriors group, other than the host and two of the other women, I did not know anyone else. But when I heard the warriors pray, my initial thought was WOW! The prayers were so powerful! I was in awe of it all! Because Debra knew I had a passion for writing poetry, she asked me to join the call and share one of my original poems that I'd shared with her and a small group of my friends previously. Although I'm an extrovert, I'd rather be in the background, making it all happen rather than in the spotlight. At that moment, I felt as if I was back on the boat and as nervous as I'd been some 40 years prior. Since I did not know the attendees on the calls, I had no prior knowledge of their life journey or knowledge of any topics that could trigger unpleasant memories. Nevertheless, I felt compelled to share my gift with the prayer warriors as they'd shared their gifts of prayer with me. I asked God for guidance and to let my words be comforting, healing, accepted, and bring about laughter, which is a natural remedy that invigorates the soul. I realized no matter where we started out or the roads we'd traveled; we were now all in the boat rowing together—fervently praying for ourselves and others.

In early 2023, Debra put together a retreat for the Prayer Warriors group. She presented me with two opportunities, which turned out to be assignments. I completely understood the first assignment and was excited to do it. She asked me to come up with items and create gift bags for the group in connection with the *"Get Out of the Boat"* theme. Since I was a zealous crafter, I was confident I could complete that assignment with ease. The second assignment, however, would cause me to get in the boat without a life vest. She asked me to be the host of the fashion show event on the closing night. Because I only knew a few of the ladies, I knew I would have to interact with and observe them during the three-day event. This way I could adequately describe their character and their outfits and personalize each as they walked the catwalk. I also needed to add in a bit of humor as the MC. I did not know what anyone would wear, so the words needed to flow with an upbeat tempo. I started out by reciting *"The Woman at the Well"* poem I'd written a few months back. The audience loved it and cheered me on, giving me the confidence and desire to complete the assignment. At that moment I knew what it meant not to lean on my own understanding but to trust and believe in His word—for **He** is the captain who will continue to lead me and guide me through turbulence, turmoil, rough seas, joys, and harvests of plenty. **He** is my solid rock and my anchor in times of sorrow and trouble.

I've learned, fear makes you sit down, FAITH makes you stand up. I still haven't learned to swim, but I now have a desire to learn because I finally know what it means to get out of the boat and faithfully walk on water!

Come on in the water's fine
Come on in, this child of mine
I have all you need to keep you afloat
So go ahead, my child, and get on the boat
For in the boat you will easily find
confidence, determination, motivation and peace of mind
No need to fret on what to pack and bring
For I AM your captain, your lord, your savior, your King
For I know what your needs are before you even ask
I'm the comforter, the healer, so go ahead and take off your mask
No need for a life vest or device to keep you afloat
You'll be totally transformed by the time you get off the boat
The things you've been afraid to say, try, or do in my name
By the time you get to the middle of the ocean, your life will no longer be the same
So cast your fears, doubts, and all uncertainty aside
Cast low self-esteem, worries, woes, and whatever else betides
I AM waiting. I will not let you falter.
"COME" it's time for you to get out the boat and walk on the water!
To God be the Glory for All Blessings!

Meet the Author | Ollie L. Lofton

Ollie L. Lofton is a native Floridian who currently resides in Orlando, Florida. She is the proud mother of two children, Colleen and Jamari. Professionally, Ollie has worked for AT&T for 37 years, serving as a Manager—a role she has used not just for leadership, but for mentorship. Over the past 28 years, she has made it her mission to encourage young people within the company to take full advantage of educational and training opportunities to enrich their lives and build lasting careers.

Beyond her professional life, Ollie is also a passionate crafter, channeling her creativity into her personal pursuits.

Over the last four years, since the onset of COVID-19, Ollie's spiritual journey has deepened. Inspired by Jeremiah 29:11—*"For I know the plans I have for you..."*—she embraced the stillness of that season and was led to the Prayer Warriors group, where she found an exceptional community of faith-filled believers. Here, Ollie continues to grow in her walk with God, sharing her story as part of her faith-filled testimony.

YOU MUST GET OUT OF THE BOAT

DR. SHARON E. HARRIS

Getting out of the boat can be hard, but God has called us to a greater purpose. We have to allow Him to use us how He pleases. Sometimes life seems so unfair, and we forget who we are and who we belong to. Jeremiah 28:11 says, the "For I know the plans I have for you declares the Lord, plans to prosper you and not harm you, plans to give you a hope and a future." The context of this promise for the Israelites was when they were under oppression and kicked out of their land. This promise was not to be fulfilled for 70 years.

Whatever God is going to do, it will be in His time. That means we must wait on God and remain faithful to Him no matter what this life brings. I had to learn that. It wasn't easy. I endured many trials and disappointments. I believed staying in the boat was safer.

...and he arose and rebuked the wind and said to the sea peace be still, the wind ceased and there was a great calm.

— MARK 4:39

For me, this verse said to stay in the boat because Jesus is there and wherever He is, there is peace. RIGHT?

The bible also states trials come to make us strong.

Strong winds blew when my 19-year-old nephew was murdered. I was in the boat. Then the rain came; my dad passed away. I was in the boat. Holding on to my faith, trusting in the Lord. He said, *"I will never leave you or forsake you."* I was strong because I was in the boat. *"I will bless the Lord at all times; his praise shall continually be in my mouth."* I stayed in the boat!

I stayed in church; I sang in the choir. I worked with the usher board. I felt safe in the boat. I had peace in the boat. I am surrounded by my church family, my sisters, my brother and friends. It's so easy to stay in the boat. The greatest storm of my life came in 2012. Our son had been diagnosed with cancer. I prayed, *"Dear God, let him live!"* He fought a good fight; he stayed the course. Then the Lord called him home. I silently cried out, *"When the storms of life are raging, Lord, please stand by me."* I prayed it was only a bad dream. As I left the hospital, I remember it being a long walk down those dark corridors, not bringing our son home. King David of the bible; He rose, washed his face when his baby boy passed. I tried to do the same. And I said, *"God, I am not strong, only you know my pain. I will continue to serve you. I am broken. How can I stay in the boat and do ministry?"* I am safe in the walls of the church. I didn't feel like I could get out of the boat. Yet the word states I can do all things through Christ who gives me strength.

I WAS BROKEN IN THE BOAT.

It was time to move. My husband decided we would move to his hometown in Florida. I thought, *Why? This is my safe place; I'm leaving my family, our daughter, grandchildren, friends, and our church.* I said to myself, *"Lord, not now."* It was December 2018. I retired and joined my husband in Florida. I said to myself, *"Where am I?"* I was in the wilderness—sitting in a boat on dry land. I felt alone. My in-laws had jobs and their families to deal with, and the visits were far and few. The people that I knew lived in other parts of Florida. Soon I felt like Jonah in the belly of the whale. My thoughts: *why am I here, Lord?* I am in a foreign land—the wilderness with no purpose, no hope. I kept thinking: *Why me? What do you want me to do?* I now know I heard the Lord say in my spirit that it was time to be renewed and restored. He told me to seek His face, walk with Him daily, and pray. Sometimes God will take you to the valleys, the wilderness, and low places.

My husband and I attended many churches but did not commit. We knew we had to be fed the word to stay nourished. We stayed connected to our home church, bible study, and prayer line.

You may ask, what all of this has to do with getting out of the boat? Well, I continued to pray. God had me isolated for a year, just Him, me, my church prayer line, and bible study. There is so much power in prayer, and God was up to something. I realized that sometimes you have to be put in situations for God to move you into your purpose. My prayer life was changing. I was praying for others profoundly. No more selfish prayers. Studying the word and praying the word moves God's heart. Believing that no weapons formed against me shall prosper, I am above and not beneath. I am the head and not the tail. Praying that all things work together for the good of them who love the Lord, who are called for His purpose. Praying—be anxious for nothing! The Lord is faithful and true to His word. My prayers were superficial until I got out of the boat.

One Sunday, I needed prayer for myself. I went to the receiving line and one mother was laying hands on the sick and praying over people. As I was next in line, she was called away and pulled me over to pray in her place!

OUT OF THE BOAT!

I don't know what happened, but the spirit of the Lord came over me as I laid hands on this young woman. The spirit moved in my heart. He spoke to her hurt and to her pains. It was like a fire in my bones.

Was I a prayer warrior? What! Me? No way. The Lord used me that day. Later, I was asked if I minded receiving prayer requests from the church to pray over? My answer was, "*Sure.*" I did not mind praying. Look at God! It was not me, but the Holy Spirit praying for God's people. I was only a vessel. Is this what the Lord wants me to do?

NEW FRIENDS AND SISTERS IN CHRIST IN THE BOAT

As I was seeking his face and wanting to meet new people, I went to a Zumba exercise class at one of the local senior centers. The Lord is always on time. I met an impressive young lady named Pat, who introduced me to Ms. Debra. We hit it right off. They welcomed me to Florida and as time went on; I noticed our conversations were always godly. We would even pray for or with one another in the parking lot! I had mentioned that I had three sisters in California and felt alone without them. These ladies became my sisters. God knows exactly what you need. I truly felt blessed and amazed at what He was doing in my life.

AUG 14, 2020 - MY ACCIDENT

My world turned upside down again! Life was good until I blacked out and fell down my stairs; God saved my life. The reason, according to the doctors, was unknown. Maybe my blood sugar dropped too low. I received seven staples in the back of my head and a spinal injury. I did not break any bones. Praise be to God. I laid in my bed for months and my vocal cords were not working right. How was I to pray? I could hardly speak. The pain in my body was unbearable, and the medication made me feel like a zombie. I told my doctor I did not like how I was feeling; I got off those heavy medications and was given Tylenol extra strength and muscle relaxers. God was with me as my therapy began. I was moving and walking slowly. One day my speech therapist had me repeat the words *"GOD IS GOOD."* What?! That was just what I needed. God is indeed good! These words helped me speak and strengthen my voice. I began by reading the Lord's prayer during prayer calls and scripture. I could not pray the way I did before—my throat would close and I would cough. Neuropathy had set in my hands and feet. I pressed my way through. One night as I lay on my bed, I thought to myself, *is this how people feel when they are alone and helpless?* I had my husband and friends praying for me. The Lord allowed me to feel like one who had no one to visit them or talk to.

OUT OF THE BOAT?

One year later, after my physical therapy and speech therapy, God called me to minister in the Advent nursing care home. This is not my plan, but I had said yes to the Lord, not knowing what I would do. I was afraid. *Dear God, help me.* My retirement plans were to travel and see the world. On my first day, the activity director had asked me to do the devotion because the Chaplin had quit! Does God know what he is doing? Well, the bible states *"I know the plans that I have for you"* all it takes is getting out of the boat. I never thought that I would be a devotional leader, a worship leader, or a prayer warrior! Where is the chaplain? I have been here for three months doing what

God has called me to do. The new chaplain came, I never met Him.

When we step into our purpose and trust God with our lives, He gets all the glory, and we get the blessings. I feel so blessed to share my life with the seniors in the facility. I love singing, praying, and showing them the love of God. I have witnessed healings and miracles in their lives, too. Debra would ask me about the nursing home, and the prayer call ministry. I shared that I really felt bless how God was using me to impact lives.

THE VISION

One morning after our exercise class, Debra told me she believed God was leading her to start a prayer line. She said that she would pray about it and would I join in with her. I She never considered herself a leader, one month she said; only for a month! Look at God. I think my friend was out of the boat too! This was the beginning of something that only God could do. On the prayer line, just hearing the praise reports of how the Lord was moving in the lives of each woman, even I was growing stronger. We shared personal testimonies, some of heart aches and heart breaks, some of love and laughter. This prayer line became a sisterhood. We felt safe and could count on one another to pray for our different situations. We not only pray, but expect God to move!

THE RETREAT

Time to get out of the boat and walk on the water.

Debra prayed about having a retreat to celebrate our years together. Yes, did I say years! It was. We immediately loved each other at this first meeting. I believe it was truly the connection that we all experienced through the prayer line each Sunday. I am mentioning this prayer line so that you can see the power of God when you step into your purpose and obey God. Whatever He has assigned your hands to do, just do it! Get out of the boat, step into the water as Peter did, and don't take your eyes off Jesus. We were all challenged to do the same at this retreat.

Many of the women have returned to school or change careers. Some of us are retired, God still can use us! If you feel it is too late for your dreams, talk to Jesus. He knows the plan for your life. I always had a desire to write a book, that was over ten years ago. I'm out of the boat! We can do all things through Christ, who gives us strength. I did not know God would use me to pray. It is me and God in the throne room. I am out of the boat! I didn't know He wanted me to love on people in the nursing home. I now have the faith to stand on His word and declare His promises. I believe in the power and the authority He has given not only me but you as well to walk on water and get out of the boat of depression, get out of the boat of oppression. You have the power of God inside of you to be all that He has ordained you to be. God has not given us the spirit of fear, but one of power, love, and a sound mind. Don't wait. It is time to live your dreams. It's time to fulfill God's purpose for your life. Step out on faith, open the restaurant, the flower shop. Walk on water, be the nurse or doctor. All your dreams are waiting to be birthed out of you! Even prayer warrior.

My faith has been tested and tried. When I had doubt or fear; Philippians 4:6,7 *'"Do not be anxious about anything but in everything by prayer and supplication with thanksgiving let your request be known to God, and the peace of God which surpasses all understanding will guard your hearts and mind in Christ Jesus."* I had to stop worrying about the how, when, where, and what. I had to let go and let GOD! I promise you He is the way maker and the promise keeper. Trust Him to lead and guide you in your purpose and in all the dreams He has put inside of you. Just get out of the boat!

I am praying for you to walk on water.

MEET THE AUTHOR | DR. SHARON E. HARRIS

Dr. Sharon E. Harris is a wife, mother, grandmother, and GG. She is a bible teacher and minister of the Gospel of Jesus Christ.

Dr. Sharon retired from Gardner Community Health Center as a Registered Dental Supervisor and a Dental Assistant Instructor in California. Dr. Sharon received her degrees from San Jose City College, San Jose Christian College, and Sacramento Bible College and Seminary. She now serves at the Solaris Nursing Care Facility in Florida and leads Saturday morning worship service and Tuesday devotionals.

Dr. Sharon enjoys serving people and leading others to Christ. In her ministry, *Rose of Sharon,* she shares her gifts of prayer, praise dance, and improv drama. When not serving you will find her at the ocean or near a lake watching the sun rise.

www.ingramcontent.com/pod-product-compliance
Lightning Source LLC
Chambersburg PA
CBHW050653160426
43194CB00010B/1924